PEARLS

FOR

DOLLARS

COMPENDIUM TO
WEALTH
&
ENTREPRENEURIAL
SUCCESS

BY: STEVE ROBERTS

Table of Contents

PREFACE

"You can have more than you've got because you can become more than you are"
-Jim Rohn-

Successful people have something in their personality that sparks interest instantaneously. They are more enthusiastic and positive than most of the people, make money while sleeping and enjoy a life full of freedom. This made me ask myself how did they do it and begin my journey on looking for answers.

These people have effectively programmed their mentality for success throughout their lives, which instantly reminds me of a successful entrepreneur that once said: "winners never feel sorry for themselves"; this always stuck with me.

One of the greatest motivational speakers, Anthony Robbins, said that our mind is two million a year old machine that is not designed to make you happy but rather designed to make you survive, explaining that the mind is always comparing things to know what we've done wrong in order to change and survive. You may have observed throughout your life that many people you know are constantly worried about many issues; they are always remembering the past, foreseeing the future and failing to live their present realities.

It's no secret our culture has actively changed since the evolution of technology and the introduction of the Internet during the last two decades. We've seen how a capitalist economy and new generations admire the rich and famous, shifting the dreams of young adult minds from pursuing secure professions to striving for newer and riskier entrepreneurship tendencies. We've also seen how many driven entrepreneurs have become experts in many fields and have achieved the highest ranks in different industries without a formal education.

How did they succeed to achieve such triumphs in such a short period of time? You may be thinking it was luck or that they are just geniuses of society. That's exactly how unsuccessful people think, they simply believe in good fortune when other people succeed, but they don't have the same beliefs about achieving their own dreams. This type of thinking is nothing more than a defense mechanism we commonly use in order to convince ourselves that we are rational, sane and will not risk ourselves to pursue dreams with unexpected results.

If you strongly think they were lucky then you might want to answer yourself the following question: How could billionaire entrepreneur Elon Musk take over the internet payment industry by creating PayPal, take over the electric automobile industry by creating Tesla, take over the renewable energy industry with Solar City and take over the space industry by creating Space-X, in just one fraction of his lifetime? Well, it simply couldn't have been luck by itself.

There were other forces working together to make all of these companies succeed. Don't get me wrong, I believe great things can also happen by just pure luck, but certainly, it was not the sole factor in this situation. Without a doubt, Elon

Musk faced great difficulties throughout the years, but in the end, he succeeded, and that's the only thing most people will remember. Although I cannot speak for him, I strongly believe he has still not forgotten about the difficult road to success, as he can still get emotional when remembering past struggles.

Studying successful entrepreneurs throughout my life has led me to identify valuable principles or pearls successful entrepreneurs possess and unsuccessful ones lack. The next few chapters are devoted to explaining these pearls in detail. Let this opportunity inspire you to become the most successful and passionate entrepreneur you can be.

PEARL 1: SECRETS TO RICHES

One of the things you have to understand is how wealthy people make money. This is one of the secrets you have to truly comprehend if you want to become a millionaire. It's also the first thing worth figuring out before doing anything at all, as everything you do after that decision will help you get there.

When you come to understand that formal education is not directly proportional to the amount of money you can make things are going to start changing your life for the better and when I mean better, I mean you will start making money. Let me ask you this question? Out of all the people you know, how many of them are wealthy right now? Really wealthy? Wealthy doesn't mean acquiring expensive cars, boats or even a beautiful and expensive house. I'm talking about those that wake up and go to sleep while constantly making money.

I bet you know very few or none at all. But why does this happen? It's simple. Some people graduate and start working for a company or maybe a business, others decided to invest a couple of more years in order to study professions such as medicine law, engineering, architecture, etc, with the goal of attaining wealth eventually. People who choose these professions may be employed or self-employed.

Being in these two categories will make you earn money, but will not let you build wealth effectively and exponentially. They commonly think that after graduating they will make sufficient money and begin saving for retirement. Nevertheless, when they achieve success and begin to make money, they start paying their loans, buying houses, expensive cars, and other things that don't help them get there.

They find themselves spending more than they produce and procrastinating on building wealth by learning to invest. For example, if you're making half a million and you're spending six-hundred thousand, then you have a deficit of one-hundred thousand which makes you basically poor.

This will become a vicious cycle throughout the rest of your career if you're not wise enough to strategize and create plans to avoid this problem. On the other hand, if you can learn how to build wealth and invest your hard-worked money in buying assets, you can build wealth progressively.

You don't necessarily have to become an entrepreneur to make money and build wealth, but if you're worried about not making enough money you should start to look for other methods which can help you get there. Ask yourself this, Do you want to work actively for money or would you prefer creating multiple sources of income? This question will guide you to understand passive vs. active income. Before explaining the types of income you need to know what assets are and what liabilities are. This knowledge will lead you to create or find effective sources of income for yourself.

Warren Buffett, one of the most successful entrepreneurs in the United States and self-made billionaire, explained the importance of having multiple sources of income if you want to create wealth.

An asset is basically something that puts money in your bank account and a liability is something that takes money away from your bank account. It's as simple as that! If you enjoy drinking coffee every day at an expensive place and you find yourself spending more than six dollars on coffee daily, then at the end of the month you're surely going to have a hundred dollars less than you would otherwise.

Yes, your coffee can be a liability, as well as the expensive food you eat. In the same way, if you like going drinking every Friday night and spending hundreds of dollars, that is also a liability. Wealthy people learn where to put their money and what purchases to avoid in they want to acquire lots of money.

For instance, those couple of hundred dollars you might save by having coffee at your house instead of periodically going out to an expensive coffee place, can be used to buy things that could put money into your bank account, such as assets. Assets are things such as industrial stocks and high-tech company stocks, owning or having part ownership of a company that makes money, acquiring gold, investing in products, and basically, anything you can acquire that will fill your bank account progressively. That is how you become rich, by acquiring numerous assets throughout your life.

Real estate is also an asset and you can become quite wealthy by acquiring properties if you do it right.

Imagine you buy a house every two years with the money you make while having a regular job. When you retire, you may have accumulated more than ten houses. You could set yourself to generate ten thousand dollars monthly just by renting properties. This will surely make you wealthy as you age.

It can be difficult in the beginning, but, as time goes by, those properties will eventually pay each other out, and you will begin to receive juicy profits that you can possibly invest in other assets. It can also help you acquire that expensive toy or liability you've always dreamed of. This is the difference between people that make a moderate amount of money and spend it on things such as cars, boats, planes versus the ones that control their urges for material acquisitions and build their wealth slowly.

Although a car is a liability, you may wish to reward yourself with it, and its fine, but if you know you're paying high amounts of monthly money on expensive toys and it's affecting your financial situation, then you should exercise urge control and set your priorities straight.

Learning to discover assets nowadays generation is not difficult at all. Using the internet, we can search for companies we wish to invest in, we can trade digital currency and stocks instantly, and we can also market ourselves to the world by using platforms such as YouTube, Facebook, Twitter, Instagram and the like. You may also wish to consider the different options available for you before starting a project. This is an invaluable opportunity you must seriously think about.

If you feel you should achieve some sort of success successful first before seeking an audience, then do it that way. You're the only one that knows what you're capable of and feels comfortable with. Other opportunities include creating online courses, writing books, doing talks and interviews, etc.

You just need to figure out your passions along your journey by attempting different things. Start searching and thinking about opportunities every day, stop living in the past, worrying about the future, and just set your mind to achieve.

PEARL 2: REPROGRAMMING
THE MIND

As you have already seen throughout your life, many people are more worried about what their parents, friends or other people may think of them instead of what they think of themselves. I know this for a fact because all of us have felt this way sometime in our lives. We keep practicing this state of mind because most of us don't know better; it's called being mentally unsuccessful. We become submissive to our minds for prolonged periods of time, which little by little alters our best state of functioning and takes us to the deepest and worst places we can imagine. Failure to break this routine is proved to be highly detrimental to our mental health, as we can think or even believe we're not good enough to achieve great success.

This state of mind limits brain potential and becomes an obstacle to future goals and dreams.

Our main purpose in life is to be creative, happy and live a good life. I believe life is not meant to make us follow a set of written rules and live passively without having a chance to change the world. If this were not true, I highly doubt we would have overcome historic problems mankind has faced since the beginning of times. The fear of failure and not believing in ourselves prevents creative people from changing the world, making an impact and creating new realities for themselves and the people around them. On the other hand, positivity is defined as the quality or state of being positive.

Positive people accept the world as it is. They simply do not complain because they don't like their present realities. Instead, they try and figure out how they can change that reality by looking for solutions. Meanwhile, negative and unsuccessful people are always in their head, thinking what if? What if this goes wrong?, what if I can't do this?, what if I fail?, what if I don't make any money?, what if I turn out to be unsuccessful. This is the language of the poor.

Poor mind habits make you over-analyze and not execute. It makes you focus on stressful thoughts and doesn't let you be free. It prefers focusing on problems rather than solutions. Eventually, this mindset will affect your opportunity to achieve. Being positive is not something easy; it's something you work on. It's way easier for you to point out problems than figuring out ways to find solutions, as this takes mental strength, courage and passion. Yet, our rational minds always find a way to lead us to negative thinking. Why do you think this happens? It's obvious.

We just spend more time practicing negativity than positivity. When you're not thinking about bad things, you can only be thinking of good things. This is the energy you have to create and release from your mind. Have you ever had something bad happen when you're having a bad day? I certainly have. Understanding the negative implications thoughts have on your reality is something unsuccessful people don't understand but the successful clearly comprehend.

Self-confidence or self-belief is not something you're born with. It's something you develop throughout the years, which can also be shaped by success or failure. Success doesn't happen quickly, it takes time, and develops day by day as you overcome difficulties and find solutions to your problems.

The only way you will create success is if you have enough dedication and willingness to solving the problem you want to solve. Practicing confidence and self-belief helps you realize that overcoming difficulties is just something you achieve by changing your perspectives for the better.

PEARL 3: BRAINSTORMING SUCCESS

We've all had a great idea in the past, an idea we've thought can turn out to be the next million-dollar breakthrough. As soon as we thought of it, we could not wait to share it with the people around us, showing them this great new idea or project. Sooner or later, you had a reality check and one of these two things possibly happened: you just found out your idea already exists or your idea did not impress the person you've just told it to. Your dream was suddenly shattered, so you rationalize, quickly forget about it and fail to work on it in order to take it to the next level.

The more ideas you have and the more you explore as a young entrepreneur, the more likely you will succeed. It will lead you to discover the thing you passionately decide to create or work on. Keep in mind that there are many mountains and buildings you can climb in your entrepreneurial journey. Selecting the projects you like the most is perhaps the most important task you need to take on before you dedicate all your energies and efforts. Exercising exploration may save you from spending the next ten years of your life on something you can, later on, find out was unsuitable for you in the first place.

So always remember, the more you can explore, the better your chances for achieving future success. Furthermore, you will learn more about yourself than you could ever imagine. It will increase your overall skill-set and entrepreneurial experience.

Those who aren't willing to explore different areas may never get to experience passion along with success, an idea many successful entrepreneurs agree on. When you finally find that thing you are passionate about and immediately think it is not profitable, you better think again. Imagining a business model instantly is not something every person can do.

Having a clear business model in place will take your idea to the next level. That idea you may have might be very useful and also provide lots of value to many people around the world without you knowing it. Before giving up on it, you might first want to think more open-minded. For instance, when Facebook was created, it obviously didn't have the same value it has now. After launching the platform on one campus, the idea began to spread, initially proving its acceptance and ultimately becoming the best social network.

It just takes time and patience. If you don't have patience and begin to doubt your idea early on, you will find yourself constantly changing ideas and not letting them evolve. Even worse, they may never get known. Another thing that can stop you from starting your project is trying to be perfect in what we want to accomplish. Without a question, perfection is important but trying to be perfect in the initial stages of your idea or project will lead to many interruptions that will get in your way and limit your creative ability.

When I was young and naive, I thought the world was perfect. Throughout the years I've seen with my own eyes how imperfect it is and how all of us have the same potential to succeed if we try our best. Eventually, that chance for success will come to those who can overcome the obstacles they face. Some people just don't think this way.

They simply think they can't achieve success, lack creativity and vision for greatness. Learning not to get influenced by others is an important skill you will have to develop throughout time. Keeping in mind that your parents, family or friends always have your best interest in you, will certainly prevent future relationship problems.

PEARL 4: PLAN BEFORE EXECUTING

One common mistake many entrepreneurs make is deciding on projects without thinking about it for more than a couple of days. This can easily lead to failure. Implementing action without passion can make you spend valuable time on something you don't truly love to do.

In fact, you may start that idea or project and fail just because your lack of passion did not make you try hard enough. Your mind might to tell you that you weren't capable and instruct you to give up entrepreneurship and move on with your normal life. Successful entrepreneurs learn to identify if they are passionate about a project soon, they accept the lack of passion early on and try to change focus onto other ideas or projects if they conclude it will be for the best.

You have to know what you're doing if you want to put yourself in the best position to succeed. If you don't know what you're doing you're never going to have the kick your ass attitude that is essential to entrepreneurship. Instead, you will feel lost, overwhelmed and not motivated. This is why understanding your skill-set is one of the most valuable things on the road for success.

Entrepreneurs usually have trouble identifying what is the first idea they want to work on. Keeping in mind that entrepreneurs involve themselves in different projects throughout their life can make you find passion in projects you wish to pursue throughout your journey, while holding on to bigger, more advanced future projects without being discouraged in the process. Involving yourself in many things can be key to finding your drives and ambitions. It will not necessarily define your destiny as an entrepreneur. Rather, you should think of your first ideas or projects as gateways to future success. It may be beneficial to create a timeline that will guide you to your ultimate goals while pursuing other projects that can help you get there.

Successful entrepreneurs are social people who enjoy listening and interacting with others. Different paths to success can give you certain types of happiness but when success is driven by helping others succeed, that will turn out to be the biggest success you can achieve.

It's important to know exactly whom you surround yourself with, as you will be the by-product of the sum of all of them. This doesn't mean you should limit your relationships, but rather, establish the limits of such relationships if you don't want their thoughts controlling your creative mind.

Negative people are filled with negative energy, which leads to negative thoughts and negative thoughts and ultimately a negative reality. Do you know anyone like this, of course, you do, they're everywhere? That's exactly why successful people interact more often with the open-minded and self-confident, which are really passionate about the idea that they can achieve great things.

Being influenced by the wrong people will limit your capabilities, eventually, lead to dissatisfaction and make you feel trapped. People who don't think like successful entrepreneurs are always thinking and solving problems with their brains which eventually will lead to nothing because they don't have the courage to take action.

Realizing these people just don't know better will inspire you to help them out of their misery before it's too late. Common scenarios like these explain why a great number of entrepreneurs have moved to other countries or states in pursuit of like-minded individuals. One of my favorite entrepreneurs, Larry Ellison, described in a graduation speech, how one day he suddenly packed his bags and left to Silicon Valley, San Francisco, in order to pursue his dreams. He didn't know exactly what he wanted to do, but he definitely knew he wasn't going to fulfill the idea his adoptive parents had of him for becoming a doctor.

Conversely, he had another dream, a bigger one, and most importantly, he had the courage to believe he was going to be successful while proving them wrong.

Some entrepreneurs might experience setbacks when other people don't believe in them, while the open-minded and passionate counterparts with strong beliefs of their potential simply just accept that reality and try to change it.

They do this because they're sure they want to change the world. So if there's something you should bear in mind is that every entrepreneur has had the same difficulties you may be currently facing, and it will continue to happen over and over again throughout history. Only the great believers can strive for success and passionately persevere until they achieve their goals.

Pearl 5: Executing like a Genius

After finding that successful project or business, you need to figure out next how you're going to be different from the competition if it already exists; and when I say different I mean better. Just because that thing you want to do already exists, doesn't mean you have to let it go.

Chances are, you can improve it, make it better, possibly beat your competition and in the worst-case scenario, coexist with them while being successful.

The importance of being passionate about your business is that it's going to make problem-solving less of a burden. It will be easier for you to be more creative and stand out from your competition. You will begin to ignore work hours and focus deeply on tasks. When you constantly solve difficult problems, they just get easier and easier.

So the main goal is to discover something you're passionate about, put in the effort and improve yourself and your project or idea constantly. If you don't combine passion with effort, chances of succeeding will become limited.

The strategies you implement can save you time, money and energy. This is a skill that is gradually developed by acquiring significant knowledge throughout your experiences and past struggles. The only way you can figure out what not to do this by making these mistakes throughout your journeys, learning them from the people who already committed them or developing observational and analytical capabilities that will help you foresee barriers.

If you want a successful strategy, you need to know exactly what is it exactly that you want in the long run, so that you can implement a series of steps that can help you get there eventually and sooner. Identifying a successful role model or mentor that has achieved what you want to achieve is crucial. You may want to learn from the things they have done in order to get there as well as the pitfalls they've experienced and you should avoid. I know this sounds pretty obvious but many people fail to do this. It's okay to be skeptical about some things but you should always do your homework and strive to figure out what other achievers have done.

If you want to build a product, first you may want to begin by identifying a specific market or group of people that you may impact and help once you have created it. After doing this, you should start studying those people so that you can learn how to target them before you introduce the product to the market. That will give you the opportunity to know exactly how you should market the product and what type of consumers or fan base you wish to address throughout the creation of your idea or project.

Chances are when you have a finished and flawless product, you will also have a strong and eager market waiting to reward you. It's called doing your homework and planning ahead. Don't just try and sell them things just to make money, as the majority of people are not naive. On the other hand, try to develop a long-term relationship with your audience or consumers, let them be part of your life, ask for constructive criticism and create for them that thing that will bring tons of value to their lives. After they get to know your product they will form their own personal opinions of your brand or company. The market will tell you soon enough if you did the right thing.

Strategies are valuable because implementing them from the start of your journey will help you solve problems easier and faster. If you think about it, entrepreneurship and business are all about solving problems. Some problems are easy but others can be quite hard. Getting past the easy ones may be simple but if you want to solve more advanced problems you should always look for help when you don't have the solutions and understand that you cannot solve everything by yourself in every situation.

If you were to try and solve everything by your own, you will soon enough find yourself out of time, and time equals money.

As an entrepreneur, you have the responsibility to improve every day. The better you eventually become the more likely you will succeed. One way to do this is by mirroring successful people you may admire and studying their habits, the way they communicate, the way they interact with people, their response to rejection and their ability to stay calm and focused when things get difficult.

Along the way, many people will be skeptical about your ambitions. If you take their criticism as a chance to improve, it will inspire you to work harder in perfecting your project or idea. That criticism you may not like may have the keys to unlocking valuable information you may need if you're looking to expand the audience or consumer crowd you wish to address.

Learning to receive criticism will make you the smarter, more business savvy and you will be on your way to becoming a respectful and humble individual that people may begin to admire. Inspiring other people to become better human beings will turn you into the best entrepreneur you can be. The fact is that people love to do business or even work for people that have this mindset. Soon enough you'll find that taking this approach to your entrepreneur life will help you grow along the way and transform you in ways you can't imagine.

www.ingramcontent.com/pod-product-compliance
Lightning Source LLC
Chambersburg PA
CBHW061447180526
45170CB00004B/1591